3

STRONG KIDS HEALTHY PLATE
Vibrant Vegetables

Katie Marsico

CHERRY LAKE PRESS

Published in the United States of America
by Cherry Lake Publishing Group
Ann Arbor, Michigan
www.cherrylakepublishing.com

Content Adviser: Debbie Fetter, PhD, Assistant Professor of Teaching Nutrition, University of California, Davis
Reading Adviser: Marla Conn, MS, Ed, Literacy specialist, Read-Ability, Inc.

Photo Credits: ©Tatevosian Yana/Shutterstock.com, front cover; ©Alexandra Lande/Shutterstock.com, 1;©Jukov studio/Shutterstock.com, 4; ©Africa Studio/Shutterstock.com, 6; ©Africa Studio/Shutterstock.com, 8; ©Alas_spb/Shutterstock.com, 10; ©USDA/ChooseMyPlate.gov, 12; ©littlenySTOCK/Shutterstock.com, 14; ©LightField Studios/Shutterstock.com, 16; ©Estrada Anton/Shutterstock.com, 18; ©CMYK/Shutterstock.com, 20

Cherry Lake Press is an imprint of Cherry Lake Publishing Group.

Library of Congress Cataloging-in-Publication Data

Names: Marsico, Katie, 1980- author.
Title: Vibrant vegetables / Katie Marsico.
Description: Ann Arbor, Michigan : Cherry Lake Publishing, 2020. | Series: Strong kids healthy plate | Includes index. | Audience: Grades K-1 | Summary: "Vegetables keep your skin healthy and help your body fight off illness. Discover the five vegetable groups that help your body to grow strong and maintain a healthy diet. Content encourages balance and making healthy choices. This level 3 guided reader is based on the U.S. government's diet recommendations. Readers will develop word recognition and reading skills while learning about food and where it comes from. Includes table of contents, glossary, index, author biographies, sidebars, and word list for home and school connection"— Provided by publisher.
Identifiers: LCCN 2020002746 (print) | LCCN 2020002747 (ebook) | ISBN 9781534168640 (hardcover) | ISBN 9781534170322 (paperback) | ISBN 9781534172166 (pdf) | ISBN 9781534174009 (ebook)
Subjects: LCSH: Vegetables in human nutrition—Juvenile literature. | Nutrition—Juvenile literature. | Children—Nutrition—Requirements—Juvenile literature.
Classification: LCC QP144.V44 M37 2020 (print) | LCC QP144.V44 (ebook) | DDC 612.3—dc23
LC record available at https://lccn.loc.gov/2020002746
LC ebook record available at https://lccn.loc.gov/2020002747

Cherry Lake Publishing Group would like to acknowledge the work of the Partnership for 21st Century Learning, a Network of Battelle for Kids. Please visit http://www.battelleforkids.org/networks/p21 for more information.

Printed in the United States of America
Corporate Graphics

Table of Contents

About the Author

Katie Marsico is an author of nonfiction books for children and young adults. She lives outside of Chicago, Illinois, with her husband and children.

What colors of vegetables do you eat?

What Are Vegetables?

Vegetables are plants or parts of a plant used for food.

What vegetables will you eat today? Perhaps you like peppers and carrots. Maybe you prefer potatoes or corn.

There are five main groups of vegetables. Dark-green vegetables are one. Broccoli and spinach are in this group. So are many kinds of lettuce.

Red and orange vegetables form the second group. Carrots and bell peppers are in it.

Starchy vegetables are another group. This group **features** corn and white potatoes.

Have you ever tried chickpeas or soybeans? They are in the peas and beans group.

The final vegetable group is all other vegetables. It includes beets and celery. Onions and mushrooms are also in it.

This beet is fresh and tastes sweet.

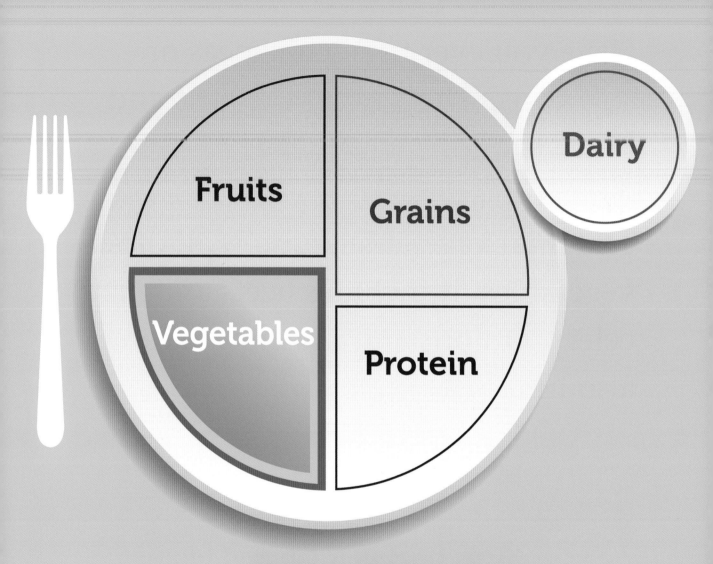

ChooseMyPlate.gov

An Important Part of Your Plate

Vegetables are one of five main **food groups**. Each group is part of a **balanced diet**.

You need a balanced diet to grow. It helps your body stay healthy.

How Do Vegetables Help?

Eating vegetables gives you **fiber**. Your body uses fiber to break down food.

Vegetables add **potassium** to your diet. Potassium keeps your heart healthy.

Vegetables are filled with **vitamins** A and C. Vitamin A keeps your skin healthy. It also helps your body fight off illness. Vitamin C is good for your skin, bones, teeth, and gums.

Dig into a Healthy Diet!

Are there enough vegetables in your diet? You should eat 1 1/2 to 2 cups (.35 to .5 liter) daily.

Don't forget there are five vegetable groups! Make sure your weekly diet includes all of them.

Be creative. Help your family find new ways to eat vegetables. Healthy eating should be tasty . . . and fun!

Glossary

balanced diet (BAL-uhnsd DYE-it) eating just the right amounts of different foods

features (FEE-churz) includes something important

fiber (FYE-bur) a substance found in vegetables that helps the body break down food

food groups (FOOD GROOPS) groups of different foods that people should have in their diet

potassium (puh-TAH-see-uhm) a substance found in vegetables that supports heart health

starchy (STAR-chee) filled with a white substance found in potatoes and certain grains such as rice

vegetables (VEJ-tuh-buhlz) plants that farmers grow for food

vitamins (VYE-tuh-minz) substances found in food that your body needs to work properly

Home and School Connection

a	diet	green	new	sure
add	dig	group	of	sweet
all	do	grow	off	tastes
also	don't	gums	one	tasty
an	down	have	onions	teeth
and	each	healthy	or	the
another	eat	heart	orange	them
are	eating	help	other	there
balanced	enough	how	part	they
be	ever	illness	peas	this
beans	family	important	peppers	to
beet	features	in	perhaps	today
bell	fiber	includes	plant	tried
body	fight	into	plate	used
bones	filled	is	potassium	uses
break	final	it	potatoes	vegetable
broccoli	find	keeps	prefer	vitamin
carrots	five	kinds	red	ways
celery	food	lettuce	second	weekly
chickpeas	for	like	should	what
colors	forget	main	skin	white
corn	form	make	so	will
creative	fresh	many	soybeans	with
cups	fun	maybe	spinach	you
daily	gives	mushrooms	starchy	your
dark	good	need	stay	

Find Out More

Book

Reinke, Beth Bence. *Why We Eat Vegetables*. Minneapolis, MN: Lerner Publications, 2018.

Website

USDA—MyPlate Kids' Place

www.choosemyplate.gov/browse-by-audience/view-all-audiences/children/kids

Use games and learning activities to find out more about vegetables and healthy eating.

Index